D1442449

Pebble®
Plus

Exploring the Seasons

Exploring Summer

by Terri DeGezelle

CAPSTONE PRESS

a capstone imprint

Pebble Plus is published by Capstone Press,
1710 Roe Crest Drive, North Mankato, Minnesota 56003.
www.capstonepub.com

Books published by Capstone Press are manufactured with paper
containing at least 10 percent post-consumer waste.

Library of Congress Cataloging-in-Publication Data
DeGezelle, Terri, 1955-
  Exploring summer / by Terri DeGezelle.
    p. cm. — (Pebble plus. Exploring the seasons)
  Includes bibliographical references and index.
  Summary: "Color photos and simple text introduce the summer season"—Provided by publisher.
  ISBN 978-1-4296-7698-4 (library binding) — ISBN 978-1-4296-7912-1 (paperback)
  1. Summer—Juvenile literature. I. Title. II. Series.
  QB637.6.D438 2012
  508.2—dc23

                                                          2011029891

Editorial Credits
Gillia Olson, editor; Sarah Bennett, designer; Svetlana Zhurkin, media researcher, Kathy McColley, production specialist

Photo Credits
Alamy: Bildagentur-online, 20 (inset), Todd Muskopf, 18–19; Capstone Studio: Karon Dubke, cover (center);
Dreamstime: Ivonne Wierink, cover (right), Photographerlondon, 20–21; Shutterstock: Arpi, 12–13, Brocreative, 5,
LianeM, 14–15, SaraJo, 16–17, silver-john, 10–11, wolfmaster13, 1

Note to Parents and Teachers

The Exploring the Seasons series supports national science standards related to earth science.
This book describes and illustrates the summer season. The images support early readers in
understanding the text. The repetition of words and phrases helps early readers learn new
words. This book also introduces early readers to subject-specific vocabulary words, which are
defined in the Glossary section. Early readers may need assistance to read some words and to
use the Table of Contents, Glossary, Read More, Internet Sites, and Index sections of the book.

Printed in the United States of America in North Mankato, Minnesota.
102011   006405CGS12

Table of Contents

Hot, Hot, Hot

In summer, the sun is hot!

It's the hottest season of the year.

In the Northern Hemisphere,

the first day of summer

is June 21 or 22.

What Causes Seasons?

As it goes around the sun,

Earth spins on a tilted axis.

Earth's tilt makes different parts

of the planet point at the sun

at different times of the year.

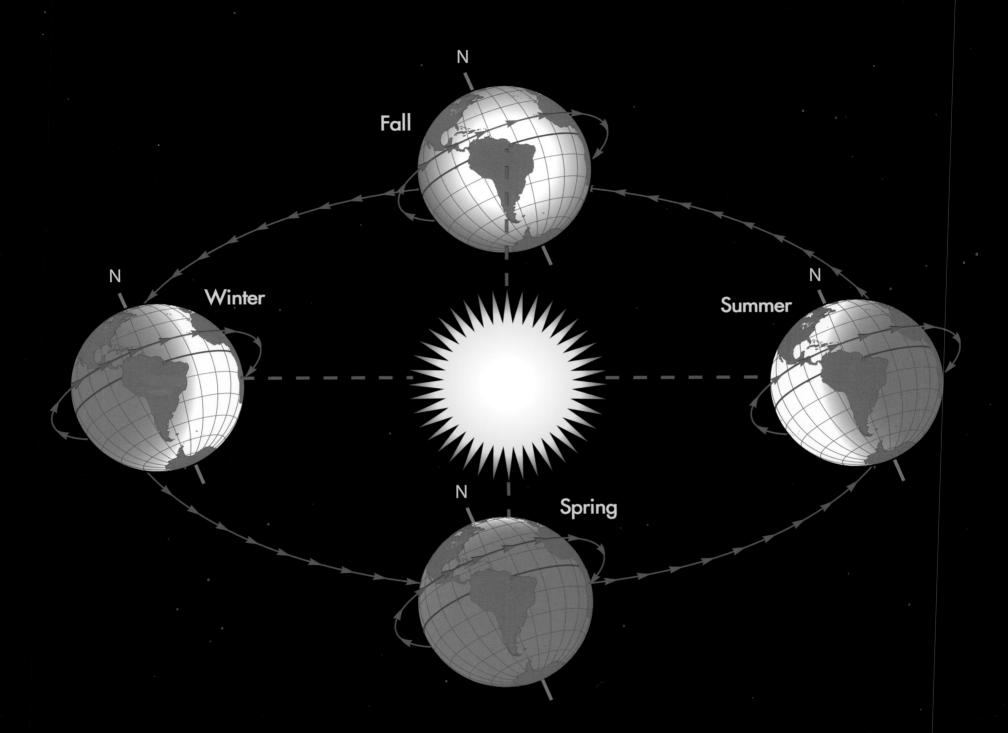

Fall

Winter

Summer

Spring

The seasons change as different parts of Earth point at the sun. Summer begins when Earth's axis points most directly at the sun.

Daylight

Daylight lasts the longest in summer. The sun's rays also shine the most directly on us. Long days and direct light bring hot temperatures.

Water in Summer

Summer weather warms lakes
and other bodies of water.
Summer brings thunderstorms.
But summer may also bring dry
weather that leads to droughts.

Trees in Summer

Plenty of sun gives trees green leaves in summer. Apples and other fruits grow on trees. Trees also grow new buds that will open next spring.

Animals in Summer

Animals can find plenty
of food in summer.
Young deer eat grasses.
Bees and butterflies gather
nectar from flowers.

People in Summer

People dress for hot activities in summer. They wear shorts and sandals. People swim to cool off. Families go camping. People play baseball.

North and South

The Northern Hemisphere's summer is the Southern Hemisphere's winter. U.S. kids enjoy summer vacation, while kids in Brazil are in school for winter.

Glossary

axis—a real or imaginary line through an object's center, around which the object turns

bud—a small shoot on a plant that grows into a leaf or a flower

drought—a long period of weather with little or no rainfall

hemisphere—one half of Earth; the Northern and Southern hemispheres experience seasons opposite to each other

nectar—a sweet liquid found in many flowers

ray—a line of light that beams out from something bright

season—one of the four parts of the year; winter, spring, summer, and fall are seasons

temperature—how hot or cold something is

tilt—leaning; not straight

Read More

Anderson, Sheila M. *Summer.* Seasons. Minneapolis: Lerner Publications, 2010.

Smith, Sian. *Summer.* Seasons. Chicago: Heinemann Library, 2009.

Winnick, Nick. *Summer.* Seasons. New York: Weigl Publishers, 2011.

Internet Sites

FactHound offers a safe, fun way to find Internet sites related to this book. All of the sites on FactHound have been researched by our staff.

Here's all you do:

Visit *www.facthound.com*

Type in this code: 9781429676984

Super-cool stuff! Check out projects, games and lots more at **www.capstonekids.com**

Index

Word Count: 218
Grade: 1
Early-Intervention Level: 21